Writing Stories
Fairy Tales

Anita Ganeri

Raintree is an imprint of Capstone Global Library Limited, a company incorporated in England and Wales having its registered office at 7 Pilgrim Street, London, EC4V 6LB – Registered company number: 6695582

www.raintreepublishers.co.uk
myorders@raintreepublishers.co.uk

Edited by Dan Nunn, Rebecca Rissman, and Sian Smith
Designed by Joanna Hinton-Malivoire
Original illustrations © Capstone Global Library 2013
Picture research by Ruth Blair
Production by Sophia Argyris
Originated by Capstone Global Library Ltd
Printed and bound in China

ISBN 978 1 406 26037 3 (hardback)
17 16 15 14 13
10 9 8 7 6 5 4 3 2 1

ISBN 978 1 406 26044 1 (paperback)
17 16 15 14 13
10 9 8 7 6 5 4 3 2 1

British Library Cataloguing in Publication Data
Ganeri, Anita, 1961-
Fairy tales. -- (Writing stories) 1. Fairy tales--Authorship--Juvenile literature. 2. Fairy tales. 3. Children's stories.
I. Title II. Series
  808.3-dc23

Acknowledgements
We would like to thank the following for permission to reproduce photographs: Shutterstock background images and design features, pp.4 (© Thomas M Perkins), 5 (© Christian Slade), 6 (© notkoo), 7 (© advent), 8 (© jordache), 9 (© wavebreakmedia), 12 (© Kiselev Andrey Valerevich), 14 (© fcarucci), 16 (© nomeko), 16 (© VectorShots), 18 (© mikeledray), 22 (© Kirill__M), 24 (© EYUP IZZET CAGLAR), 26 (© Featureflash)

Cover photographs reproduced with permission of Shutterstock: castle (© Elena Schweitzer), rainbow (© Lori Giles), tree/flowers (© Mayovskyy Andrew), fairies (© AnastasijaD), crown (© Ivan Ponomarev), stars (© Flame of life).

Every effort has been made to contact copyright holders of material reproduced in this book. Any omissions will be rectified in subsequent printings if notice is given to the publisher.

Some words are shown in bold, **like this**. You can find out what they mean by looking in the glossary.

Contents

Follow this symbol to read a fairy tale.

Writing a story

A story is a piece of **fiction** writing. It tells the reader about made-up people, places, and events. Anyone can write a story! What you need is a **setting**, some **characters**, and a **plot**.

You can write different types of stories.
There are mystery stories, silly stories,
adventure stories, scary stories, animal
stories, and many others. This book is
about writing fairy tales.

What is a fairy tale?

A fairy tale is a **fictional** story. Many fairy tales have **characters** such as fairies, princesses, dragons, giants, and elves. Popular **settings** for fairy tales are castles and palaces, woods, or magical lands.

How many fairy tale characters do you recognise?

The **plot** of a fairy tale often tells of the struggle between two sides, such as good and evil, or rich and poor. A fairy tale usually has a happy ending. What is your favourite fairy tale?

Getting ideas

Before you start writing, you need to get some ideas. Ideas may come from your imagination or from another fairy tale that you have read. You might start with an idea for an interesting **character**, or an exciting twist to the **plot**.

A good way to remember your ideas is to jot them down in a notebook. Keep it with you all the time. Then you can scribble down anything that comes into your head, even if it is just a few words.

What's the plot?

What happens in your fairy tale? This is called the **plot**. It needs a beginning, a middle, and an end. You can use a **story mountain**, like the one below, to help you plan your plot.

Middle
The main action happens. There may be a problem for one of your characters.

Beginning
Set the scene and introduce your main **character**.

Ending
The problem is solved and the story ends.

Your story starts at one side of the mountain, goes up to the top, then down the other side.

A **timeline** is another good way of working out a plot. Mark the story's main events along the timeline. Here is a timeline for the fairy tale told in this book.

Princess forgets how to laugh.

⬇

King tries everything to cheer her up.

⬇

Magician comes to palace.

⬇

Tickles princess with feather and makes her laugh.

⬇

Magician is prince in disguise.

⬇

Princess and prince fall in love.

⬇

Princess marries prince.

Once upon a time

The beginning of your story is very important. This is where you introduce your main **character**. It needs to grab your readers' attention so that they want to keep reading.

Can you turn any of these ideas into story starters?

- A princess is put under a spell.
- A mermaid loses her magical shell.
- A giant falls down a bottomless well.

A Fairy Tale

Once upon a time, there lived a princess. She was very pretty and very kind. But she was always sad. A wicked witch had put a spell on her. The spell made the princess forget how to laugh.

 Many fairy tales start with "Once upon a time…".
Can you think of a different beginning?

Setting the scene

Setting the scene means deciding on the place and time in which your story is set. It tells your reader where and when the story happens. A glittering palace, like the one below, makes a great **setting** for a fairy tale.

The princess lived in a glittering palace. The palace had dainty towers and turrets that soared into the sky. All around were lovely gardens, filled with sweet-smelling flowers. It was the most beautiful place to live in the whole world.

Can you think of any other settings for your fairy tale?

Making up characters

Your story needs strong **characters** that your reader believes in and cares about. Think about what sort of people they are, what they look like, and how they are feeling. Jot down the details in fact files.

Character fact file
Character: princess
Looks like: pretty; with long, dark hair
Sounds like: musical voice
Personality: kind; helpful
Likes: kittens; cupcakes; pink shoes
Dislikes: not being able to laugh

Character fact file
Character: wicked witch
Looks like: long, pointed nose; straggly hair
Sounds like: hard, cackling voice
Personality: cruel; mean; vain
Likes: toads; spells; herself
Dislikes: pretty princesses

The princess and the wicked witch are the main characters in our story.

With her sparkling eyes and long, dark hair, the princess was the prettiest girl in the kingdom. She was also the kindest. Everybody loved her. Everybody, that is, except the wicked witch. The witch was old and cruel, and she hated the princess for being so nice.

 Can you think up good names for the princess and the wicked witch?

 17

The middle

The middle of your story is where the main action happens. This is where something goes wrong for one of your **characters**, or they have to try to solve a tricky problem. Here are some problems that your fairy-tale characters might face.

The character...
- is turned into a frog
- gets lost in the woods
- falls into a deep sleep
- is tricked
- falls under a spell.

Can you think of any other problems?

The wicked witch hated the princess so much that she put her under a spell. The spell could only be broken if someone made the princess laugh.

"That'll show her," the witch cackled. "She won't look so pretty if she's always sad. No one will want to marry her now!"

What tricky problem does the princess have?

Mind mapping

It can be hard to think what happens next in your story. If you get stuck, try doing some **mind mapping** to help you move the **plot** along. Write down one key word or thought. Then jot down any connected words or thoughts that come into your head.

Don't spend too long on your mind map. A few minutes will do.

Putting on a funny show.

Giving her a kitten.

What might cheer up the princess?

Singing a silly song.

Tickling her with a feather.

Making the witch disappear.

Everyone tried to make the princess laugh. The king gave her a kitten but that didn't work. The queen sang her a silly song but that didn't work either. The princess's little sister put on a funny show. But nothing made the princess laugh.

Use the ideas from your mind map to keep the plot flowing.

Using speech

Try using **dialogue** in your story. Dialogue means the words that people say. Dialogue shows what your **characters** are thinking and feeling. It helps to bring your story to life.

"It's no good," sighed the king. "We'll just have to try something else."

Put **speech marks** around the words that are spoken.

"It's no good," sighed the king. "We'll just have to try something else."

"But we've tried everything," said the queen, sadly. "What else can we do?"

The king put his head in his hands and thought hard.

"I know," he said. "I'll offer a reward to anyone who can make her laugh. That should do the trick."

Dialogue is also good for breaking up long chunks of text.

Exciting writing

When you are describing your **characters** or **setting**, choose your words carefully. This will make your writing more exciting. You can add describing words called **adjectives** to explain what things are like and **adverbs** to describe the way things are done.

Slowly, he pulled a large, purple feather from his sleeve.

Slowly is an adverb. *Large* and *purple* are adjectives.

One day, a magician arrived at the palace. He wore a dazzling coat of silver and gold. Slowly, he pulled a large, purple feather from his sleeve. He tickled the princess gently under her chin. The princess's mouth twitched. Then she smiled. Then she laughed a long, tinkling laugh.

How many adjectives and adverbs can you spot in the story?

Fairy-tale ending

You have reached the end of your story. This is the place where you need to tie up all the loose ends. The ending tells your reader what has happened to your **characters** and how they have solved any problems they had.

They all lived happily ever after.

Most fairy tales end happily and the characters' wishes come true.

The spell was broken! Now, the princess couldn't stop laughing. Her family were delighted. The king offered the magician a reward.

"I'd like to marry the princess," said the magician, who was really a handsome prince in disguise.

The princess said yes at once. So, the prince and princess got married and lived happily ever after.

Can you think of a different ending to the story?

More top tips

1 Read lots of fairy tales by other writers. This will help to spark off ideas and give you a good feel for this type of story writing.

2 Read your story out loud to see if it sounds right. This can be particularly helpful when you are writing **dialogue**.

3 Be ready to rewrite your story several times before you are completely happy with it. This is what lots of writers do.

4 Try making a **story mountain** using a well-known fairy tale, such as *Little Red Riding Hood*. This will help you to plan your own story.

5 Tell your story from a different point of view to make it more interesting. For example, you could use the princess's voice.

6 Even though you are writing a fairy tale, make your **characters** believable. Put yourself in their shoes and think about what you would do or say.

Glossary

adjectives describing words that tell you about a noun (a noun is a naming word)

adverbs describing words that tell you about a verb (a verb is a doing word)

characters people in a piece of writing

dialogue words that characters say

fiction piece of writing that is about made-up places, events, and characters

fictional about made-up places, events, and characters

mind mapping thinking of everything you can about a subject

plot what happens in a story

setting time and place in which a story is set

speech marks marks that show the words someone has spoken

story mountain mountain-shaped diagram that helps you to plan out a story

timeline list of events in the order in which they happen

Find out more

Books

How to Write Stories, Celia Warren (QED
  Publishing, 2008)
Writing Stories, Anita Ganeri (Raintree
  Publishing, 2013)
Write Your Own Story Book, Louie Stowell and
  Jane Chisholm (Usborne Publishing, 2011)

Websites

**www.bbc.co.uk/schools/ks2bitesize/english/
writing**
Learn how to improve your writing skills on this
website.

**www.readwritethink.org/files/resources/
interactives/cube_creator/**
The writing cubes on this website will help you
to create your own stories.

Index